CREVE COEUR PUBLIC LIBRARY DISTRICT

DATE DUE	

Super Simple
Walk & Run

Healthy & Fun Activities to Move Your Body

Nancy Tuminelly

Contributing Physical Education Consultant, Linn Ahrendt, Power Play Education, Inc.
Consulting Editor, Diane Craig, M.A./Reading Specialist

A Division of ABDO

ABDO
Publishing Company

visit us at www.abdopublishing.com

Published by ABDO Publishing Company, a division of the ABDO Group, P.O. Box 398166, Minneapolis, Minnesota 55439. Copyright © 2012 by Abdo Consulting Group, Inc. International copyrights reserved in all countries. No part of this book may be reproduced in any form without written permission from the publisher. Super SandCastle™ is a trademark and logo of ABDO Publishing Company.

Printed in the United States of America, North Mankato, Minnesota

052011
092011

 PRINTED ON RECYCLED PAPER

Editor: Liz Salzmann
Content Development: Nancy Tuminelly, Linn Ahrendt
Cover and Interior Design and Production: Colleen Dolphin, Mighty Media, Inc.
Photo Credits: Colleen Dolphin, Shutterstock

Library of Congress Cataloging-in-Publication Data

Tuminelly, Nancy, 1952-
  Super simple walk & run : healthy & fun activities to move your body / Nancy Tuminelly
     p. cm. -- (Super simple exercise)
  ISBN 978-1-61714-964-1
  1. Physical fitness for children--Juvenile literature. 2. Walking--Juvenile literature. 3. Running--Juvenile literature. I. Title.
  GV443.T867 2012
  613.7'042--dc22

2011000977

Super SandCastle™ books are created by a team of professional educators, reading specialists, and content developers around five essential components—phonemic awareness, phonics, vocabulary, text comprehension, and fluency—to assist young readers as they develop reading skills and strategies and increase their general knowledge. All books are written, reviewed, and leveled for guided reading, early reading intervention, and Accelerated Reader® programs for use in shared, guided, and independent reading and writing activities to support a balanced approach to literacy instruction.

Note to Adults

This book is all about encouraging children to be active and play! Avoid having children compete against each other. At this age, the idea is for them to have fun and learn basic skills. Some of the activities in the book require adult assistance and/or permission. Make sure children play in appropriate spaces free of objects that can cause accidents or injuries. Stay with children at the park, playground, or mall, or when going for a walk. Make sure children wear appropriate shoes and clothing for comfort and ease of movement.

Contents

Time to Walk & Run!

Being active is one part of being healthy. You should move your body for at least one hour every day! You don't have to do it all at one time. It all adds up.

Being active gives you **energy** and helps your body grow strong. There are super simple ways to move your body. Two of them are walking and running. This book has fun and easy activities to get you started. Try them or make up your own.

Do You Know?
Being Active Helps You

1 be more relaxed and less stressed

2 feel better about yourself and what you can do

3 be more ready to learn and do well in school

4 rest better and sleep well at night

5 build strong bones, **muscles**, and joints

So turn off the TV, computer, or phone. Get up and start walking and running!

Muscle Mania

You have **muscles** all over your body. You use them whenever you move any part of your body. The more you move your muscles, the stronger they get!

shoulder

arm

neck

stomach

chest

back

upper leg

lower leg

Healthy Eating

You need **energy** to move your body. Good food gives your body energy. Some good foods are fruits, vegetables, milk, lean meat, fish, and bread. Foods such as pizza, hamburgers, French fries, and candy are okay sometimes. But you shouldn't eat them all the time.

Remember!

- ☑ Eating right every day is as important as being active every day

- ☑ Eat three healthy meals every day

- ☑ Eat five **servings** of fruits and vegetables every day

- ☑ Eat healthy snacks

- ☑ Eat fewer fast foods

- ☑ Drink a lot of water

- ☑ Eat less sugar, salt, and fat

Move It Chart

Make a chart to record how much time you spend doing things. Put your chart where you will see it often. This will help you remember to fill it out every day. See if you move your body at least an hour each day.

Move It Chart
Week of March 8-14

Activity	Sunday	Monday	Tuesday	Wednesday	Thursday	Friday	Saturday
basketball	●		●	●	●		●
Whistle Play	●					●	
clean the windows			●			●	

1 Put the title of your chart at the top of a piece of paper. Then put "Week of" and a line for the dates.

2 Make a chart with eight **columns**. Put "activity" at the top of the first column. Put the days of the week at the top of the other columns. Under "activity," list all of the things you do. Include sports, games, and **chores**. Don't forget the activities in this book! Put "total time" at the bottom. Make copies of the chart.

3 Start a new chart each week. Put the dates at the top.

4 Mark how much time you spend on each activity each day. Be creative! Use different colors, **symbols**, or clock faces. For example, a blue sticker could mean 15 minutes of movement. A purple sticker could mean 60 minutes of movement.

○ = 10 minutes   ○ = 30 minutes
● = 15 minutes   ● = 60 minutes

5 Add up each day's activity. Did you move your body at least an hour every day?

Tools & Supplies

Here are some of the things you will need to get started.

music player

masking tape

rubber bands

rubber gloves

tongs

stopwatch

plastic bag

fabric paints

box

music

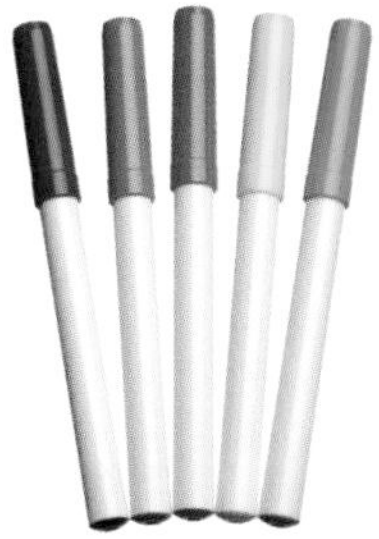

markers

whistle

large plastic hoop

rope

dustpan

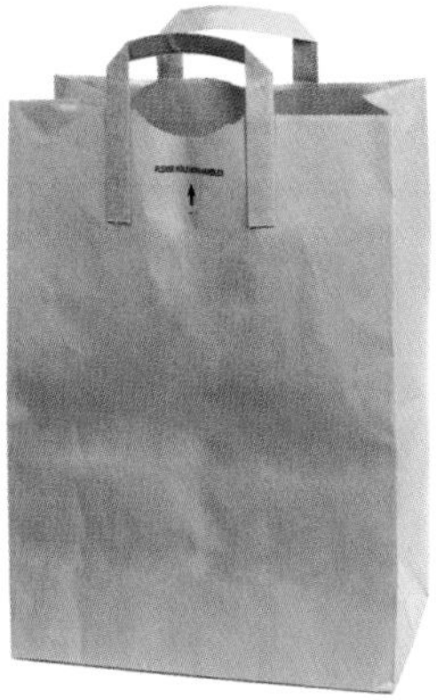

paper bag

water bottle

towels

chair

jump rope

athletic shoes

Total Body Walk

You use over 200 muscles when you walk!

WHAT YOU NEED

athletic shoes
water bottle

MUSCLES USED

leg
arm
shoulder
back

TIME

10-30 minutes

1. Stand tall. Take a few deep breaths. Hold your stomach tight. Begin walking. Take **normal** steps. Swing your arms from your shoulders.

2. Put your hands on your shoulders. When you take a step, push your arms straight out. When you take the next step, bring your hands back to your shoulders.

3. Bend your arms with your fists at your shoulders. Keep your elbows at your sides. When you take a step, **punch** your arms straight over your head. When you take the next step, bring your fists back to your shoulders.

4. Put one hand on your shoulder. Hold your other arm straight out to the side. When you take a step, bend the straight arm and touch your shoulder. Stretch the bent arm out straight. When you take the next step, **switch** arms.

Neat Neighborhood

Have fun walking and cleaning up at the same time!

WHAT YOU NEED

paper or plastic bags
rubber gloves
tongs
dustpan
markers
paper
tape

MUSCLES USED

leg
arm
back

TIME

10-60 minutes

1. Get a group of friends or family members together. Make sure an adult knows where you are going. Choose a nearby park, your neighborhood, or a playground. As you walk, pick up litter.

2. Safety first! Stay away from streets. Wear gloves. Do not pick up the trash with your bare hands.

3. Be extra careful when picking up glass or sharp objects. Use tools such as tongs or a dustpan.

4. Try sorting recyclables as you pick them up. Use markers to label the bags.

5. Do it every week! Invite other friends to join the fun. See who can pick up the most trash!

➡ Make club T-shirts to show what you are doing!

15

Stairs Everywhere

Make climbing stairs a fun hike everywhere you go!

WHAT YOU NEED

inside or outside stairs
athletic shoes
notebook
pen

MUSCLES USED

leg
arm

TIME

5-10 minutes

1 Choose a set of stairs at your home or school. Climb up the stairs.

2 Then climb down. Count how many steps you climb. Try to climb more stairs every time.

3 Find other places to climb stairs. Use the stairs instead of elevators or **escalators**.

4 Find a tall building. See if you are allowed to go up the stairs. Count the steps. How long did it take?

5 Keep a journal. Write down where and when you climb. Keep track of how many steps you climb and how long it takes. Climb stairs with your friends to see who can go faster!

✋ Make sure it is safe to use the stairs in these places. You may need an adult with you.

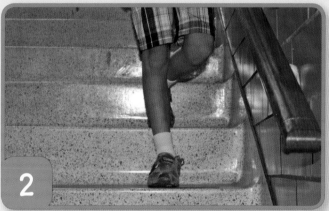

CLIMBING JOURNAL
DAY 5
Where: school
When: 3:30 p.m.
How many steps: 64
Time: 5 minutes
DAY 6

Whistle Play

Take turns whistling and moving!

WHAT YOU NEED

whistle for each person

MUSCLES USED

leg
arm

TIME

10–15 minutes

1. Have everyone spread out and walk around.

2. Grin and wave at each other. Take giant steps. Then take baby steps.

3. Take turns blowing the **whistles**. Everyone has to do what each number of whistle blows means. Use the ideas below or think up your own.
   - 1 whistle blow means run around.
   - 2 whistle blows means skip around.
   - 3 whistle blows means form a circle and walk 10 steps to the left.
   - 4 whistle blows means hop around and then walk 10 steps to the right.

➡ Whistles are loud, especially if you are inside. Make sure you are not bothering anyone else!

Scavenger Walk

For outside on a sunny day or inside on a rainy day!

WHAT YOU NEED

paper

pen or pencil

paper bag for each person

markers

MUSCLES USED

leg

arm

back

TIME

15–60 minutes

1. Make a list of 10 to 15 things to look for on a walk. If you're going outside, include things such as leaves, sticks, rocks, cans, and bottles. If you're staying inside, include things such as pens, spoons, coins, crayons, and shoes. Make a copy of the list for each person.

2. Decorate your paper bag with markers.

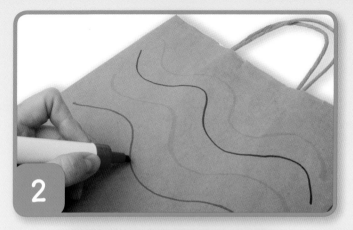

3. Walk around and look for the things on the list. Bend down, lean over, reach, and grab. Put the things you find in the bag.

4. When you find something, check it off the list.

5. After you find everything on the list, run back to where you started. See who gets done first! Or set a time limit. See who finds the most things before the time is up.

SCAVENGER
✓ Pen
✓ Spoo
gr

Spy Hunt

Use your mind and muscles on a sunny day!

WHAT YOU NEED

paper or a notebook
pen or pencil

MUSCLES USED

leg

TIME

10-30 minutes

1. Grab some paper and pen or pencil and start looking around!

2. Look for things that begin with each letter of the alphabet. Write down the things you see.

3. Try walking different ways to make it more fun! Walk on your tiptoes. Walk quickly. Walk slowly. Walk sideways.

➡ On a rainy day, play the Spy Hunt game inside! Ask an adult to take you and your friends to the mall.

A-B-C LIST
A = apple tree
B = bird
C = car
D = dog

Rag Tag

It's tag using rags!

WHAT YOU NEED

rags or towels
paper bag
sticks, rope, or tape
music player
music

MUSCLES USED

leg
arm

TIME

10-20 minutes

1. Mark off an area for the activity with sticks, rope, or tape.

2. Have everyone tuck a rag or **towel** in his or her pocket or waistband.

3. Start the music. Run around and try to grab another player's rag. Try to keep other players from grabbing your rag.

4. When you get someone's rag, put it in the paper bag. That player must take a rag out of the bag. Then he or she can keep trying to take someone else's rag.

5. Continue until the music stops. Try other moves like skipping or hopping. Or jump around like a frog!

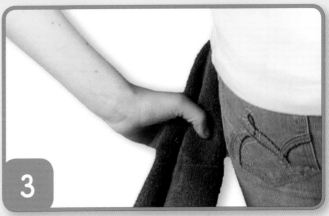

Bag Skate

Skate for a gold medal!

WHAT YOU NEED

large plastic bags
rubber bands
music player
music

MUSCLES USED

leg
arm
shoulder
back

TIME

10-30 minutes

1. Find an area with nothing in the way. Put a plastic bag over each foot. Have an adult help you put a rubber band around each ankle. They will hold the bags on. Make sure the rubber bands aren't too tight.

2. Scoot your feet across the floor like you are skating.

3. Skate forward and backward. Try making circles and figure eights. Spin around on one foot.

4. Now try speed skating! See how fast you can skate from one point to another. If there is more than one skater, have a race!

5. Put on a show. Make up your own skating moves to music. Skate dance with a **partner**. See how many different moves you can create.

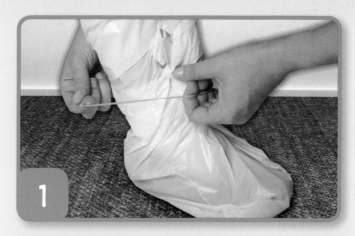

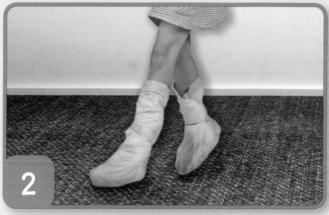

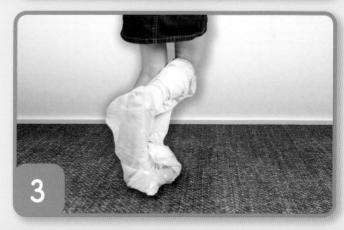

27

Obstacle Run

See how fast you can finish this course!

WHAT YOU NEED

paper
markers
tape
2 jump ropes
4 large plastic hoops
3 boxes
2 chairs
timer or stopwatch

MUSCLES USED

leg
arm
shoulder
back

TIME

10-30 minutes

1 Find a large open space. Make the following **obstacles**.
- Lay down two pieces of rope to jump over.
- Set out the **hoops** to jump or step in.
- **Stack** cardboard boxes for players to kick down.
- Put the chairs out to run around.

2 Make START and FINISH signs. Put them at the beginning and the end of the course.

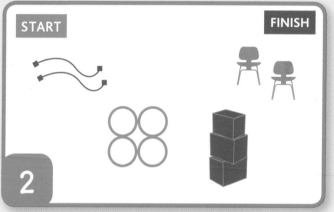

3 Now take turns running the obstacle course. Time each other to see how long you take. Try to go as fast as you can!

Just Keep Moving!

Try these during TV and homework breaks, after meals, or any time.

Red Light, Green Light

When someone calls "green light," everyone starts running across the room. Everyone stops when they hear "red light." Anyone who doesn't stop goes back to the start. See who gets to the other side first.

Walk the Dog

Take your dog for a walk around the block. It gets you outside and moving.

Crab Walk

Sit on the floor with your knees bent. Put your feet flat on the floor and your hands on the floor behind you. Lift your hips and move around the room backwards or sideways.

Walkathon

Set up a walking course around the house. Set a timer for a few minutes. See who can get the farthest before the timer goes off.

Being active is for everyone!

- Ask your family to join in activities at home.
- Have relay races with your classmates at recess.
- Have an adult take you to a safe park to play tag with friends.

Super Simple Moves
Pledge

I promise to be active and move my body for one hour a day, five days a week.
I know that eating right and getting enough sleep are also important.
I want to be healthy and have a strong body.

I will:

☑ keep track of my activities on a Move It Chart or something like it

☑ ask my friends to stay active with me and set up play times outside three days a week

☑ ask my family to plan a physical activity one day a week

☑ limit my time watching TV and using the computer, except for homework

☑ get up and move my body during TV commercials and homework breaks

To print a pledge certificate, go to www.abdopublishing.com.
For more information about being active, please visit www.letsmove.gov.

31

Glossary

chore – a regular job or task, such as cleaning your room.

column – one of the vertical rows in a table or chart.

energy – the ability to move, work, or play hard without getting tired.

escalator – a set of stairs that move, so people stand on them to go up or down.

hoop – a large ring.

muscle – the tissue connected to the bones that allows body parts to move.

normal – healthy, usual, or most common.

obstacle – something that is in the way.

partner – someone you do something with, such as dance or work on a project.

punch – to hit with a closed fist.

serving – a single portion of food.

stack – to put things in a pile.

switch – to change from one thing to another.

symbol – an object or picture that stands for or represents something.

towel – a cloth or paper used for cleaning or drying.

3-1-13